How To Become A Successful Young Man

Instructor's Manual

Diamond D. McNulty

Copyright © 2016 Diamond McNulty
All rights reserved
ISBN-10: 1-945318-00-7
ISBN-13: 978-1-945318-00-9
"Taking Over The World" – McNulty International, LLC

Pages within this book should not be reproduced without written permission from McNulty International, LLC. All rights reserved.

DEDICATION

This manual is dedicated to all of the instructors around the world who strive to make a difference everyday. This book was requested from Parents, Teachers, Principles, and Organizational Leaders from all over. It has also been demanded by Directors of Educational Institutions who believe that the "How To Become A Successful Young Man" book and workbook is a much-needed tool in our school systems today. I am an advocate for success and through this journey I have found great fulfillment in my purpose. Thank you for expressing your needs, they have assisted me in creating one of the biggest impacts in the world today.

Anything is possible!

"Giving vision to the youth – Spreading love to the world"

- Diamond McNulty

Pages within this book should not be reproduced without written permission from McNulty International, LLC. All rights reserved.

How To Become A Successful Young Man Instructor's Manual — 2016

WELCOME

Welcome to the "How To Become A Successful Young Man" Instructor's Manual. I created this book and its entirety based off of my own teaching techniques that allowed me to connect with everyone around the world no matter what age or nationality. This manual will give you access into my mind and heart. It is important that we not only want the best for our families and ourselves but we also want the best for our entire community as well. Success is not easy but it's possible. Let's all take a moment to reflect on our own dreams in life and find ways to fulfill our destiny.

INSTRUCTORS PLEDGE

Dear Diamond D. McNulty, I _____ believe in success. I will impart this material to the best of my abilities and teach it as if I created it myself. I believe the world can be better and I will be part of the solution. I understand that the two most important things I could ever offer my students are love and opportunity. My motivation is _____ and for that reason I will never give up. Aside from teaching I will assist in opening doors for all of my students which will allow them to prosper in life. Due to my dedication the world will be made better, and the highest honor I will ever receive is knowing that because of me the next generation has a chance to excel in life. I too will learn and strive to accomplish all of my personal goals in life. It is never to late to achieve anything. I believe anything is possible.

_____   _____

Print: Date:

_____

Signature:

_____

Witness

    Please take a photo of this page after signing, then post and tag us on our Facebook

Pages within this book should not be reproduced without written permission from McNulty International, LLC. All rights reserved.

page at www.facebook.com/successfulyoungman with #SuccessfulYoungMan #IamSuccessful #TheBeginningOfMySuccessJourney

How To Become A Successful Young Man Instructor's Manual | 2016

"Tell me and I forget, Teach me and I may remember, Involve me and I Learn."

- Benjamin Franklin

Message to the Instructor:

As the instructor of this course, I want to thank you for taking on the responsibility to guide our students on a positive path in life. We as leaders must not only teach but we must also care about each student on a personal level. Every student is different so we must have the ability to adapt to the different ways students learn. Be open to adapting your teaching style to a style that you as a teacher may not be familiar with. As the world changes there are so many talented kids with abilities that we have never seen before! With that said lets have fun and learn from them just as much as they learn from us.

Understanding:

Some students will have problems in certain areas and it is our job to understand what they need help with and give them the help they need. Teaching in areas of poverty or not, there are children who want to become successful. Therefore, without a shadow of a doubt it is our duty to plant the seeds that will manifest in their hearts and provide them the fuel needed to strive for greatness.

One of the greatest things we can give any child is an **Opportunity**.
One of the greatest things we can give any child is **Love**.

These two intangible things are very vital in the development of our youth today. Many kids rarely experience love from the adults around them and/or are given the opportunities to propel them from their current circumstances. Be a reliable yet knowledgeable source for kids to expand themselves and obtain the necessary answers needed to succeed.

Breakdown:

This manual is broken down into daily readings and exercises. This will allow you to engage the students and spark their interest towards excelling in life. Everyday our goal is for you to show up motivated and ready to motivate the kids to strive for greatness. Teach them ways to search for answers outside of the class as well as inside the classroom. Conduct open discussion forums that will allow you to gain insight on the students. Based on these forums, we ask that

you keep a weekly or monthly log of their progress throughout the course and submit at the end of the entire program.
throughout the course.

Engage the parents:
There is a huge separation between the school system and the household. Inside this manual we have bridged the gap to get guardians more involved. Use the materials provided to help plant the seed that will develop a child's potential to make a difference in today's society. We can't do it alone – Reach Home!

How To Become A Successful Young Man Instructor's Manual | 2016

This entire Success Program will consist of 9-12 classroom sessions, 1-2 hours each.
Every day the Instructor has homework that will prepare them for class the next day.

Review every lesson the day before.

Tools needed to perfect this course:
Daily Prizes – Give Away (Snacks, $5 Gift cards Etc.) Set a budget
Reward Program Prizes – Order our curriculum kit online. (Includes Everything)
Sign-in/Point Log Sheets (Back of book)

Pre & Post Assessment
(Download and print hardcopies or have every student complete it online at www.McNultyInternational.com)

Reward Program:

Everyday there will be three Top M.A.S (Most Active Students) winners that will receive prizes based on a performance point system. At the end of the course, all workbooks and all success plans will be turned in. All points will be tallied up which will include the completion of the workbook assignments, attendance and participation of each student. At the end of the course there will be three winners that will be chosen and awarded. Please remember to return workbooks and success plan to all students.

Top (3) Winners

1st Place - Receives a Success Plan Winner (Trophy) & A Success Medal of Honor.
2nd Place – Receives a Successful Medal of Honor.
3rd Place – Receives a Successful Medal of Honor.
Note: Every student will receive a Certificate of Completion after the complete program.

Final Wrap Up

It is my idea to have a huge celebration at the end of every success course whether it is a pizza party, bowling or roller-skating. At the ceremony all of the points throughout the entire course will be tallied up and the three winners will be announced at this ceremony. The winners will be presented with the 1st, 2nd and 3rd place prizes.

Pages within this book should not be reproduced without written permission from McNulty International, LLC. All rights reserved.

At the end of the entire course please hold a mandatory meeting with all parents to discuss the class and go over stats on each student. Therefore, together we can guide the child on the correct path of purpose. Understanding and communication from educational facilities to home is very important, and I want to highly express the importance of participation from everyone. Remember it takes a village to raise a child. Have a blessed day. Thank you!

DAY 1: INTRODUCTION

1. Fill out daily sign-in log
2. Give the Pre-Assessment to every student. Collect from all students, copy and place in envelope or have them complete it online.

Today is a fundamental day for you to get to know every child that you will be teaching on a personal level. The book "How To Become A Successful Young Man" will be introduced but it will not be used today. The first two things you will want to do is introduce yourself and give the kids some insight on <u>who you are</u> and <u>why they should listen</u> to you. Ask questions that will spark their interest. Prior to the class do your own personal research on success and how you view/define it. Explain to the students the importance of achieving goals in life. Remember this class will set the precedence for the entire course.

- **Instructor -** Introduce Yourself:
  _____
  _____
  _____

- **3 Key points on why kids should listen to you.**
  1. _____
  2. _____
  3. _____

  Give them the ins and outs of what they will LEARN over the next couple of weeks:

  Over the next few weeks we will be reading from the "How To Become A Successful Young Man" book while working in the workbook presented. By the time we are finished every student will have their success plan fully completed and will be ready to take over the world. I want to thank every student who is participating in this class, we will have a lot of fun.

- **Introduce the Author:** The author Diamond McNulty who wrote this book/workbook has not only figured out the key to success, but cares enough to also give you some of the secrets to life and how to achieve anything you want. Diamond McNulty is an Author, Entrepreneur, Executive Chef, Photographer, Videographer, Film Editor, Graphic and Web Designer and the list goes on. He has worked many jobs while attending school at the same time he started writing these books in the middle of the night because his

Pages within this book should not be reproduced without written permission from McNulty International, LLC. All rights reserved.

spirit just would not let him sleep. Does anybody in here have big dreams in life that will not let them sleep? How many in here want to take care of their family and have unlimited access to money/resources needed to soar in life? Great! Well you are in the right class today.

Daily Notes

How To Become A Successful Young Man Instructor's Manual | 2016

First Question of the day: Ask the class…. What is Success?

Have 3-5 students around the room answer the question and then have one of them define it based on the dictionary definition.

- **Define Success:**
_____
_____
_____

{Give the Authors Definition of Success}

<u>Diamond McNulty Definition of Success</u>:

Achieving a set level of accomplishments… accomplishing your goals.

Day 1: Questions To Ask

1. **What does everyone want to become in life?** Go through everyone in the class and fill out the class log with everyone's main career goal and backup career choices.

2. **Does anyone know how to become what you are trying to become?** For those who raise their hand, listen to them all and capture the first three of the volunteers who gets the closest to the correct response and give them a prize for trying. Tell them the lesson behind trying. – Even if you don't know the answer… It never hurts to try.

3. **Who do you know personally that is already on the career path that you picked?** Call on (3) students who gave answers to the first two questions.

Can anyone name any successful people that they know? What makes them successful? This question will spark a lot of interest. Give them insight on their parents who take care of them everyday. Successful Mothers, Fathers etc. Not just sports stars, rich and wealthy individuals. Success is more than money.

Pages within this book should not be reproduced without written permission from McNulty International, LLC. All rights reserved.

4. **Would you consider yourself already successful?** Many students are already successful because they have made it this far. What you want to do is explain that there are levels to success. Each level has different things that they will need to accomplish and goals that will need to be set. Tell them this is just the beginning and that in their life they should look to accomplish as many things as they can. Strive to be more and do more in life, for their family (parents and younger siblings) and their community.
5. **How have you benefited your community?** Have anyone volunteered with local organizations, helped younger kids with homework etc. We are looking to find ways kids want to help and are willing to help in the community.

Note from Author: One of my mentors changed my thinking in one day when he said "Diamond I'm not impressed by these wealthy folks… don't get confused because some of them might just be Big Time Losers. They might have money but their families might hate them. They could be very bad people. You want to be successful but you also want to be a good person." – *Reginald Grand 'Pierre*

WRAP UP DAY 1

- Go over the pre-assessment questions.
- Tally up the points for Day 1 and let the students know about the homework for the next meeting.
- Give away top 3 prizes for the day – Let them pick from a bag of candy or healthy snacks… something simple.
- Thank all the students for their participation.

HOMEWORK FOR DAY 2

Bring in one success quote that you like and write why you chose the quote and what it means to you. This assignment is worth - **(4 points)**

5 points if your parent or guardian signs it.

END OF DAY

How To Become A Successful Young Man Instructor's Manual | 2016

"In order to teach one must first learn. In order to learn one must listen."

– **Diamond McNulty**

DAY 2: WHEN I GROW UP

1. Fill out daily sign-in log
2. Collect and check off everyone who brought homework from **Day 1**:

Book: Chapter 1
Workbook: Read Intro - Sign Pledge.

Read Instructions: Today we will start reading the book and go over the beginning portion of the workbook. Whatever you do not finish here today will be homework for you on our next class.

Open Books
In this section you will need (9) readers: Each reader receives 3 points each.

Student Read: Dedication
Teacher Read: The Table of Contents: Ask questions to gauge their ideas on what they think the chapters will be about.
Student Read: Acknowledgement
Student Read: Special Thanks & How This Book Became
Student Read: Preface
Student Read: Chapter 1 all the way up to page 5 (Second Question)
Student Read: Up to page 6 (Third Question)
Student Read: Up to Page 8 (Plan)
Student Read: Finish Page 9 (Decision Making)
Student Read: Decision Making and Short Story

Chapter Review: Teacher read/ask student's questions – Fill out together.
Give 2 points per answer to each student.

Great Job Everyone!

Pages within this book should not be reproduced without written permission from McNulty International, LLC. All rights reserved.

Open Workbook:
In this section you will need two readers: Each reader receives 3 points each.

- **Student Read:** Dedication
- **Student Read:** My Success Pledge

Wrap up Day 2

- **Everyone sign pledge** - Take a picture of every young man holding up his signed pledge.
- Tally up the points for Day 2 and let the students know about the homework for the next meeting.
- Give away top 3 prizes for the day – Let them pick from a bag of candy or drinks… something simple.
- Thank all the students for their participation.

Congratulate everyone on finishing up the first section of the curriculum.
Give every child the chance to present the homework. (2 points per presentation)

Homework for Day 3

Complete the workbook up to page 13. **(4 Points)**

5 points if your parent or guardian signs it.

END OF DAY 2

Day 3: FRIENDSHIPS & PLANNING

1. Fill out daily sign-in log
2. Collect workbooks and check off everyone who brought homework from **Day 2**:

2 points for partially completed
4 points for fully completed without signature
5 points for fully completed with signature

Book: Chapter 2
Workbook: Exercise (Write the plan) Page 15-17.

Read Instructions: Today we will start reading chapter 2 Bro's Boyz and your Crew and do the exercise on pages 15-17 inside the workbook. Whatever you do not finish here today will be homework for you on our next class.

Open Books
In this section you will need (4) readers: Each reader receives 3 points each.
(Give the kids a chance that didn't read yesterday)

Student Read: Surrounding Friendships
Student Read: Don't Burn Bridges
Student Read: Your Future Circle
Student Read: Short Story

Chapter Review: Teacher read/ask students questions – Fill out together.
Give 2 points per answer to each student.

Day 3 – Questions To Ask

1. **How many students in here have Entertainment Oriented friends?** Talk about it (Ask them how many)
2. **How many students have Business Oriented Friends?** Talk about it (Ask them how many)
3. **How many have both Entertainment and Business Oriented Friends?** Great! Talk about it (Ask them how many)

4. **Looking at burning bridges… What ways can someone burn a bridge?** Talk about it
5. **Has anyone in here ever burned a bridge?** Talk about it
6. **Has anyone ever burned a bridge with you?** Talk about it

Daily Notes

7. **Is anyone in here already building your future success circle?** If so, ask who is in their circle and their plan breakdown and vision for those people and why.
8. **How many in this class are surrounded by gangs and drugs?** By being surrounded by it how do you take the good and leave the bad? Will you fall into the bad trap or do you plan on becoming successful?

Instructor - Tell your own story related to the chapter _____
_____
_____
_____
_____

Great Job Everyone!

Wrap up Day 3

Congratulate everyone on finishing up the second section of the curriculum.
Give every child the chance to present the homework. (2 points per presentation)
Exercise Pg. 15-17

- Tally up the points for Day 3 and let the students know about the homework for the next meeting.
- Give away top 3 prizes for the day – Let them pick from your selection... something simple.
- Thank all the students for their participation.

Homework for Day 4

Complete the workbook page 19 - 22. **(4 Points)**

5 points if your parent or guardian signs it.

Tomorrow we will play a game called **"Mr. Know It All"** with the spelling and definitions of the 50 vocabulary words that every successful person should know.

END OF DAY 3

Pages within this book should not be reproduced without written permission from McNulty International, LLC. All rights reserved.

Pages within this book should not be reproduced without written permission from McNulty International, LLC. All rights reserved.

Day 4: Make The Choice

1. Fill out daily sign-in log
2. Collect workbooks and check off everyone who brought homework from **Day 3**:

2 points for partially completed
4 points for fully completed without signature
5 points for fully completed with signature

Book: Chapter 3
Workbook: Introduce Debt Free lifestyle for homework.

Read Instructions: Today we will start reading chapter 3 make the choice and complete the debt free exercise on pages 23 -26 inside the workbook. Whatever you do not finish here today will be homework for you on our next class.

(Create a 5 min Discussion related to the following questions)

1. ***Start today off asking: What are habits?* _____.** Ask a student to look up the definition and read it out loud.
2. *Are having habits a good thing or a bad thing?* _____.
3. *Give me 3 Good habits?* _____.
4. *Give me 3 Bad habits?* _____.

Open Books
In this section you will need (7) readers: Each reader receives 3 points each.
(Give the kids a chance that didn't read yesterday)

Student Read: Destroy Bad Habits
Student Read: Stay Out Of Trouble
Student Read: Wait To Have Kids
Student Read: 5 Reasons Why
Student Read: Finish School – Build A Career
Student Read: Find the right person
Student Read: Short Story

Pages within this book should not be reproduced without written permission from McNulty International, LLC. All rights reserved.

Chapter Review: Teacher read/ask student's questions – Fill out together.
Give 2 points per answer to each student.

Ok Let's Play "Mr. Know It All"

We will divide the class up into two teams (Team A - Team B)

One person on each team will be competing against one member of the other team in a head to head match up of spelling and definition of vocabulary words. First you will choose a leader for each team. This leader will be considered Mr. Know It All for their team.
A flip of the coin determines who goes first. You will call one student on both teams to stand while you ask the starting team to spell a word and give the definition. If the first team gets it right then you will ask the second team another word with chances for both teams to make points. If the starting team gets it wrong then the opposing team is asked the same word and definition with chance to steal. If both teams get it wrong then Mr. Know It All on both teams get a chance to save the day but will only receive ½ the points. Once all words are finished there is one more chance for the other team to catch up.

Steal The Show

In the bonus round there are 10 words from the teacher that will be chosen. This is the only time where you can forfeit your Mr. Know It All title and let another team member steal the show for you. Mr. Know It All will stand head to head battle to win the game. They will be separated from their team and will be presented with a blank piece of paper and pencil.

The instructor will call out the 10 words one-by-one and each student is required to write down the correct spelling of the word and the definition. Once all words are called they have the chance to ask the teacher to repeat any of the 10 words and turn in their paper. The teacher will tally up the final score and announce it to the class. All members of the winning team will receive 3 points added to their performance score and Mr. Know It All will receive 5 points.

Great Job Everyone!

Wrap up Day 4

Congratulate everyone on finishing up the third section of the curriculum.

Ask the class question 1 & 2 inside the workbook and leave the rest for homework.

Pages within this book should not be reproduced without written permission from McNulty International, LLC. All rights reserved.

- Tally up the points for Day 4 and let the students know about the homework for the next meeting.
- Give away top 3 prizes for the day – Let them pick from your selection… something simple.
  Thank all the students for their participation.

Homework for Day 5

Complete the rest of the workbook page 23-26. **(4 Points)**

5 points if your parent or guardian signs it.

Tomorrow we will go over How To Establish A Debt Free Lifestyle

END OF DAY 4

Day 5: All About Respect

1. Fill out daily sign-in log
2. Collect workbooks and check off everyone who brought homework from **Day 4**:

2 points for partially completed
4 points for fully completed without signature
5 points for fully completed with signature

Book: Chapter 4 – All About Respect
Workbook: Low Expense Budget for tomorrows homework.

Read Instructions: Today we will start reading chapter 4 All About Respect, go over the homework and go over the Low Expense Budget on pages 27 inside the workbook. Whatever you do not finish here today will be homework for you on our next class.

Open Books
In this section you will need (7) readers: Each reader receives 3 points each.
(Give the kids a chance that didn't read yesterday.)

Student Read: Gaining Respect
Student Read: Show Respect To Others
Student Read: Respect Women
Student Read: Core Values
Student Read: Relationships
Student Read: Respect All People
Student Read: Short Story

Chapter Review: Teacher read/ask student's questions – Fill out together.
Give 2 points per answer to each student.

Great! Let's Go Over the Homework.

Pages within this book should not be reproduced without written permission from McNulty International, LLC. All rights reserved.

How To Establishing A Debt Free Lifestyle

3. On page 23 – Name five additional causes of debt? Point out five different students to give you answers. Give me one each.

4. On page 23 - Name five ways to overcome debt? Point out five different students to give you answers. Give me one each.

#5. On page 23 - Can you live without debt? Ask the class and get different opinions to see how their thought process is. Tell them to remember – **Cash is King** – if you have cash you don't need credit.

Great Job Everyone!

Wrap up - Day 5

Congratulate everyone on finishing up the fourth section of the curriculum.

- Tally up the points for Day 5 and let the students know about the homework for the next meeting.
- Give away top 3 prizes for the day – Let them pick from your selection... something simple.
- Thank all the students for their participation.

Homework for Tomorrow - Day 6

Complete the Low Expense Budget of the workbook page 27. **(4 Points)**

5 points if your parent or guardian signs it.

Tomorrow we will go over Low Expense Budget.

END OF DAY 5

Day 6: Fundamentals To Know & Practice

1. Fill out daily sign-in log
2. Collect workbooks and check off everyone who brought homework from **Day 5**:

2 points for partially completed
4 points for fully completed without signature
5 points for fully completed with signature

Book: Chapter 5 – Fundamentals to know and practice
Workbook: Dig Deeper pages 29 – 35.

Read Instructions: Today we will start reading chapter 5 fundamentals to know & practice and go over the homework and inside the workbook. Whatever you do not finish here today will be homework for you on our next class.

Open Books
In this section you will need (4) readers: Each reader receives 3 points each.
(Give the kids a chance that didn't read yesterday)

- Define Fundamentals? _____. Ask a student to look it up and read the definition out loud.

  Do Not Give the Answer until after: Fundamental is the principle on which something is based.

Student Read: Reading
Student Read: Self-Motivation & Persistence
Student Read: Faith and Motivation
Student Read: Short Story
Chapter Review: Teacher read/Ask student's questions – Fill out together.
Give 2 points per answer to each student.

Great! Let's Go Over the Homework.

How To Create A Low Expense Budget

Pages within this book should not be reproduced without written permission from McNulty International, LLC. All rights reserved.

- What is a budget? Ask the class
- Go around the classroom and ask multiple students how much do you spend per month? Let them explain their budget and write down what they spend their money on most.
- Ask them where do they get their money from?

Create five questions for the class that you would like to talk about from what they spend the most money on, about saving and do they like budgets or not. Allow a free flowing discussion and take notes.

- _____
- _____
- _____
- _____
- _____

Notes:

_____
_____
_____

Great Job Everyone!

Wrap up - Day 6

Congratulate everyone on finishing up the fifth section of the curriculum.

- Tally up the points for Day 6 and let the students know about the homework for the next meeting.
- Give away top 3 prizes for the day – Let them pick from a bag of candy or drinks… something simple.
- Thank all the students for their participation.

Homework for Tomorrow - Day 7
Complete the Lets Dig Deeper portion of the workbook page 29-35. **(4 Points)**
5 points if your parent or guardian signs it.
END OF DAY 6

Pages within this book should not be reproduced without written permission from McNulty International, LLC. All rights reserved.

Day 7: The Journey To Success

1. Fill out daily sign-in log
2. Collect workbooks and check off everyone who brought homework from **Day 6**:

2 points for partially completed
4 points for fully completed without signature
5 points for fully completed with signature

Today's Agenda
Book: Chapter 6 – The Journey to success
Workbook: Dig Deeper pages 29 – 35.

Read Instructions: Today we will start reading chapter 6 The Journey To Success and go over the homework inside the workbook. Whatever you do not finish here today will be homework for you on our next class.

- **What is Financial Literacy?** _____. Ask a student to look it up and read it out loud.

  Do Not Give the Answer until after: Financial literacy is the ability to understand how money works in the world: how someone manages to earn or make it, how that person manages it, how he/she invests it (turn it into more) and how that person donates it to help others.

- **What is Money Management?** _____. Ask a student to look it up and read it out loud.

Do Not Give the Answer until after: Money Management is the process of budgeting, saving, investing, spending or otherwise in overseeing the cash usage of an individual or group.

Open Books
In this section you will need (5) readers: Each reader receives 3 points each.
(Give the kids a chance that didn't read yesterday)

Student Read: Develop Leadership

Pages within this book should not be reproduced without written permission from McNulty International, LLC. All rights reserved.

How To Become A Successful Young Man Instructor's Manual | 2016

Student Read: Leaders Lead
Student Read: Education & Financial Literacy
Student Read: Learn To Network
Student Read: Short Story

Chapter Review: Teacher read/ask student's questions – Fill out together.
Give 2 points per answer to each student.

Great! Let's Go Over the Homework.

Go around the classroom one by one asking all the questions within Lets Dig Deeper. Even though you will ask all the questions, below I have listed key questions for you to take notes on for further observations.

Let's Dig Deeper Notes:

2. What Obstacles do you face that could stop you from becoming successful?

_____
_____
_____
_____
_____
_____
_____

3. Do you have any bad habits?

_____
_____
_____
_____
_____
_____
_____

Pages within this book should not be reproduced without written permission from McNulty International, LLC. All rights reserved.

5. Do your teachers care about you?
_____
_____
_____
_____
_____

6. What do you feel you are missing that can help you become successful?
_____
_____
_____
_____
_____

7. What are your biggest fears?
_____
_____
_____
_____
_____

8. Do you feel your school is preparing you to become successful?
_____
_____
_____
_____
_____

Further Chapter Discussion

So today we have talked about multiple things from developing leadership and building your network. I want to end the day off with two questions.

1. Does everyone in here consider himself a leader?

2. Is everyone in here building your network (Team) to help you take over the world?

Let the discussion roll with open hearts and minds. Take notes!

_____
_____
_____
_____

Great Job Everyone!
Wrap up - Day 7

Congratulate everyone on finishing up the sixth section of the curriculum.

- Tally up the points for Day 7 and let the students know about the homework for the next meeting.
- Give away top 3 prizes for the day – Let them pick from a bag of candy or drinks... something simple.
- Thank all the students for their participation.

Homework for Tomorrow - Day 8
Write a 1-page paper about where you see yourself in 5 years. **(4 Points)**

5 points if your parent or guardian signs it.

Tomorrow everyone will present in front of the class.

END OF DAY 7

Pages within this book should not be reproduced without written permission from McNulty International, LLC. All rights reserved.

How To Become A Successful Young Man Instructor's Manual | 2016

Day 8: Thinking Big

1. Fill out daily sign-in log
2. Collect workbooks and check off everyone who brought homework from **Day 7**:

2 points for partially completed
4 points for fully completed without signature
5 points for fully completed with signature

Today's Agenda
Book: Chapter 7 – Easy As 1, 2, 3
Workbook: Where I Am pg. 37 – 43.

Read Instructions: Today we will start reading chapter 7 Easy as 1,2,3 and then allow everyone a chance to present their homework. Whatever you do not finish here today will be homework for you on our next class.

Open Books
In this section you will need (5) readers: Each reader receives 3 points each.
(Give the kids a chance that didn't read yesterday)

Student Read: Think Big
Student Read: Create And Follow Your Goals
Student Read: Growth
Student Read: Stick To The Plan
Student Read: Short Story

Chapter Review: Teacher read/ask student's questions – Fill out together.
Give 2 points per answer to each student.

Writing the Vision
This chapter is the beginning stages to expanding your vision on how you should "Think Big," As a child you have the ability to use your imagination to become very creative. I want you all to be very creative in thinking about where you are now and where you see yourself in the next 5, 10, and even 20 years from now.

How To Become A Successful Young Man Instructor's Manual | 2016

Review Workbook Homework

I want to go over the homework today with you to answer any questions that you might have. We are getting to the meat of success and it is very crucial that everyone understands. No Question is a stupid question as we are all looking for answers. Even as the instructor, I have questions that I have to find the answers to but together we can make it happen. We are a family! Let's respect everyone and be mindful that the person sitting right next to you could be the next one to make a huge difference in the world.

Where I am and where I want to be - Page 37

- Take 5 minutes to fill out as much as you can, look over all the questions and ask any questions. Once the time is up we can begin by having everyone present their homework from last night in front of the class.
- Take questions and start homework presentations.
- Finish Presentations.

Great Job Everyone!

Wrap up - Day 8

Congratulate everyone on finishing up the sixth section of the curriculum.

- Tally up the points for Day 8 and let the students know about the homework for the next meeting.
- Give away top 3 prizes for the day – Let them pick from a bag of candy or drinks… something simple.
- Thank all the students for their participation.

Homework for Tomorrow - Day 9
Finish "Where I am and where I want to be" pg. 37 - 47. **(4 Points)**
5 points if your parent or guardian signs it.
Tomorrow we will finish the last chapter in the book, create vision boards and take a post assessment to the full course.

END OF DAY 8

Pages within this book should not be reproduced without written permission from McNulty International, LLC. All rights reserved.

How To Become A Successful Young Man Instructor's Manual | 2016

Day 9: Becoming A Success

1. Fill out daily sign-in log
2. Collect workbooks and check off everyone who brought homework from **Day 8**:

2 points for partially completed
4 points for fully completed without signature
5 points for fully completed with signature

Today's Agenda
Book: Chapter 8 – Becoming A Success
Workbook: Vision Board page 49

Read Instructions: Today we will start reading chapter 8 Becoming A Success and then allow everyone a chance to present their homework.

Open Books
In this section you will need (4) readers: Each reader receives 3 points each.
(Give the kids a chance that didn't read yesterday)

Student Read: The Mind For Success
Student Read: Page 90
Student Read: Page 91 - The Secret To Success
Student Read: The Secret To Success
Student Read: Short Story

The whole class reads, "Repeat After Me" together.

Chapter Review: Teacher read/ask student's questions – Fill out together.
Give 2 points per answer to each student.

Great Job Everyone!

Pages within this book should not be reproduced without written permission from McNulty International, LLC. All rights reserved.

How To Become A Successful Young Man Instructor's Manual — 2016

Wrap up - Day 9

Congratulate everyone on finishing up the final section of the curriculum.

- Tally up the points for Day 9 and let the students know about the homework for the next meeting.
- Give away top 3 prizes for the day – Let them pick from a bag of candy or drinks… something simple.
- Thank all the students for their participation.
- Work on the vision board exercise – There are many ways to create a vision board please use what best fits your needs.

- **Give the Post-Assessment to every student.** Collect from all students, copy and place in envelope or have them complete it online at www.McNultyInternational.com.

Remember! Final Wrap Up

It is my idea to have a huge celebration at the end of every success class whether it be a pizza party, bowling or skating night out. At the ceremony all of the points throughout the entire course will be tallied up and the three winners will be announced at this ceremony. The winners will be presented with the 1st, 2nd and 3rd place prizes.

At the end of the entire course please hold a mandatory meeting with all parents to discuss the class and go over stats on each student. Therefore, together we can guide the child on the correct path of purpose. Understanding and communication from educational facilities to home is very important, and I want to highly express the importance of participation from everyone. Remember it takes a village to raise a child. Have a blessed day. Thank you!

Pages within this book should not be reproduced without written permission from McNulty International, LLC. All rights reserved.

How To Become A Successful Young Man Instructor's Manual — 2016

	Name	Main Career Goal	Backup Career Choice	2nd Backup Career Choice
1				
2				
3				
4				
5				
6				
7				
8				
9				
10				
11				
12				
13				
14				
15				
16				
17				
18				

Pages within this book should not be reproduced without written permission from McNulty International, LLC. All rights reserved.

How To Become A Successful Young Man Instructor's Manual | 2016

19				
20				
21				
22				
23				
24				
25				
26				
27				
28				
29				
30				
31				
32				
33				
34				
35				
36				
37				
38				

Pages within this book should not be reproduced without written permission from McNulty International, LLC. All rights reserved.

	Name	Date	Course Day	Homework Points	Participation Y or N	Parent Participation	Daily Score
1							
2							
3							
4							
5							
6							
7							
8							
9							
10							
11							
12							
13							
14							
15							
16							
17							
18							

Pages within this book should not be reproduced without written permission from McNulty International, LLC. All rights reserved.

How To Become A Successful Young Man Instructor's Manual | 2016

19							
20							
21							
22							
23							
24							
25							
26							
27							
28							
29							
30							
31							
32							
33							
34							
35							
36							
37							

Pages within this book should not be reproduced without written permission from McNulty International, LLC. All rights reserved.

How To Become A Successful Young Man Instructor's Manual 2016

	Name	Date	Course Day	Homework Points	Participation Y or N	Parent Participation	Daily Score
1							
2							
3							
4							
5							
6							
7							
8							
9							
10							
11							
12							
13							
14							
15							
16							
17							
18							

Pages within this book should not be reproduced without written permission from McNulty International, LLC. All rights reserved.

How To Become A Successful Young Man Instructor's Manual 2016

19							
20							
21							
22							
23							
24							
25							
26							
27							
28							
29							
30							
31							
32							
33							
34							
35							
36							
37							

How To Become A Successful Young Man Instructor's Manual | 2016

	Name	Date	Course Day	Homework Points	Participation Y or N	Parent Participation	Daily Score
1							
2							
3							
4							
5							
6							
7							
8							
9							
10							
11							
12							
13							
14							
15							
16							
17							
18							

Pages within this book should not be reproduced without written permission from McNulty International, LLC. All rights reserved.

How To Become A Successful Young Man Instructor's Manual — 2016

19							
20							
21							
22							
23							
24							
25							
26							
27							
28							
29							
30							
31							
32							
33							
34							
35							
36							
37							

Pages within this book should not be reproduced without written permission from McNulty International, LLC. All rights reserved.

How To Become A Successful Young Man Instructor's Manual | 2016

	Name	Date	Course Day	Homework Points	Participation Y or N	Parent Participation	Daily Score
1							
2							
3							
4							
5							
6							
7							
8							
9							
10							
11							
12							
13							
14							
15							
16							
17							
18							

Pages within this book should not be reproduced without written permission from McNulty International, LLC. All rights reserved.

19							
20							
21							
22							
23							
24							
25							
26							
27							
28							
29							
30							
31							
32							
33							
34							
35							
36							
37							

How To Become A Successful Young Man Instructor's Manual 2016

	Name	Date	Course Day	Homework Points	Participation Y or N	Parent Participation	Daily Score
1							
2							
3							
4							
5							
6							
7							
8							
9							
10							
11							
12							
13							
14							
15							
16							
17							
18							

Pages within this book should not be reproduced without written permission from McNulty International, LLC. All rights reserved.

19							
20							
21							
22							
23							
24							
25							
26							
27							
28							
29							
30							
31							
32							
33							
34							
35							
36							
37							

How To Become A Successful Young Man Instructor's Manual — 2016

	Name	Date	Course Day	Homework Points	Participation Y or N	Parent Participation	Daily Score
1							
2							
3							
4							
5							
6							
7							
8							
9							
10							
11							
12							
13							
14							
15							
16							
17							
18							

Pages within this book should not be reproduced without written permission from McNulty International, LLC. All rights reserved.

How To Become A Successful Young Man Instructor's Manual | 2016

19							
20							
21							
22							
23							
24							
25							
26							
27							
28							
29							
30							
31							
32							
33							
34							
35							
36							
37							

Pages within this book should not be reproduced without written permission from McNulty International, LLC. All rights reserved.

How To Become A Successful Young Man Instructor's Manual — 2016

	Name	Date	Course Day	Homework Points	Participation Y or N	Parent Participation	Daily Score
1							
2							
3							
4							
5							
6							
7							
8							
9							
10							
11							
12							
13							
14							
15							
16							
17							
18							

Pages within this book should not be reproduced without written permission from McNulty International, LLC. All rights reserved.

19							
20							
21							
22							
23							
24							
25							
26							
27							
28							
29							
30							
31							
32							
33							
34							
35							
36							
37							

Pages within this book should not be reproduced without written permission from McNulty International, LLC. All rights reserved.

How To Become A Successful Young Man Instructor's Manual | 2016

	Name	Date	Course Day	Homework Points	Participation Y or N	Parent Participation	Daily Score
1							
2							
3							
4							
5							
6							
7							
8							
9							
10							
11							
12							
13							
14							
15							
16							
17							
18							

Pages within this book should not be reproduced without written permission from McNulty International, LLC. All rights reserved.

How To Become A Successful Young Man Instructor's Manual | 2016

19							
20							
21							
22							
23							
24							
25							
26							
27							
28							
29							
30							
31							
32							
33							
34							
35							
36							
37							

Pages within this book should not be reproduced without written permission from McNulty International, LLC. All rights reserved.

How To Become A Successful Young Man Instructor's Manual — 2016

	Name	Date	Course Day	Homework Points	Participation Y or N	Parent Participation	Daily Score
1							
2							
3							
4							
5							
6							
7							
8							
9							
10							
11							
12							
13							
14							
15							
16							
17							
18							

Pages within this book should not be reproduced without written permission from McNulty International, LLC. All rights reserved.

How To Become A Successful Young Man Instructor's Manual | 2016

19							
20							
21							
22							
23							
24							
25							
26							
27							
28							
29							
30							
31							
32							
33							
34							
35							
36							
37							

How To Become A Successful Young Man Instructor's Manual | 2016

	Name	Date	Course Day	Homework Points	Participation Y or N	Parent Participation	Daily Score
1							
2							
3							
4							
5							
6							
7							
8							
9							
10							
11							
12							
13							
14							
15							
16							
17							
18							

Pages within this book should not be reproduced without written permission from McNulty International, LLC. All rights reserved.

How To Become A Successful Young Man Instructor's Manual | 2016

19							
20							
21							
22							
23							
24							
25							
26							
27							
28							
29							
30							
31							
32							
33							
34							
35							
36							
37							

Pages within this book should not be reproduced without written permission from McNulty International, LLC. All rights reserved.

How To Become A Successful Young Man Instructor's Manual | 2016

	Name	Date	Course Day	Homework Points	Participation Y or N	Parent Participation	Daily Score
1							
2							
3							
4							
5							
6							
7							
8							
9							
10							
11							
12							
13							
14							
15							
16							
17							
18							

Pages within this book should not be reproduced without written permission from McNulty International, LLC. All rights reserved.

19							
20							
21							
22							
23							
24							
25							
26							
27							
28							
29							
30							
31							
32							
33							
34							
35							
36							
37							

Pages within this book should not be reproduced without written permission from McNulty International, LLC. All rights reserved.

How To Become A Successful Young Man Instructor's Manual — 2016

	Name	Date	Course Day	Homework Points	Participation Y or N	Parent Participation	Daily Score
1							
2							
3							
4							
5							
6							
7							
8							
9							
10							
11							
12							
13							
14							
15							
16							
17							
18							

Pages within this book should not be reproduced without written permission from McNulty International, LLC. All rights reserved.

19							
20							
21							
22							
23							
24							
25							
26							
27							
28							
29							
30							
31							
32							
33							
34							
35							
36							
37							

Pages within this book should not be reproduced without written permission from McNulty International, LLC. All rights reserved.

How To Become A Successful Young Man Instructor's Manual | 2016

	Name	Date	Course Day	Homework Points	Participation Y or N	Parent Participation	Daily Score
1							
2							
3							
4							
5							
6							
7							
8							
9							
10							
11							
12							
13							
14							
15							
16							
17							
18							

Pages within this book should not be reproduced without written permission from McNulty International, LLC. All rights reserved.

How To Become A Successful Young Man Instructor's Manual — 2016

19							
20							
21							
22							
23							
24							
25							
26							
27							
28							
29							
30							
31							
32							
33							
34							
35							
36							
37							

Pages within this book should not be reproduced without written permission from McNulty International, LLC. All rights reserved.

	Name	Date	Course Day	Homework Points	Participation Y or N	Parent Participation	Daily Score
1							
2							
3							
4							
5							
6							
7							
8							
9							
10							
11							
12							
13							
14							
15							
16							
17							
18							

Pages within this book should not be reproduced without written permission from McNulty International, LLC. All rights reserved.

19							
20							
21							
22							
23							
24							
25							
26							
27							
28							
29							
30							
31							
32							
33							
34							
35							
36							
37							

Pages within this book should not be reproduced without written permission from McNulty International, LLC. All rights reserved.

How To Become A Successful Young Man Instructor's Manual — 2016

	Name	Date	Course Day	Homework Points	Participation Y or N	Parent Participation	Daily Score
1							
2							
3							
4							
5							
6							
7							
8							
9							
10							
11							
12							
13							
14							
15							
16							
17							
18							

Pages within this book should not be reproduced without written permission from McNulty International, LLC. All rights reserved.

19							
20							
21							
22							
23							
24							
25							
26							
27							
28							
29							
30							
31							
32							
33							
34							
35							
36							
37							

Pages within this book should not be reproduced without written permission from McNulty International, LLC. All rights reserved.

How To Become A Successful Young Man Instructor's Manual — 2016

	Name	Date	Course Day	Homework Points	Participation Y or N	Parent Participation	Daily Score
1							
2							
3							
4							
5							
6							
7							
8							
9							
10							
11							
12							
13							
14							
15							
16							
17							
18							

Pages within this book should not be reproduced without written permission from McNulty International, LLC. All rights reserved.

19							
20							
21							
22							
23							
24							
25							
26							
27							
28							
29							
30							
31							
32							
33							
34							
35							
36							
37							

Pages within this book should not be reproduced without written permission from McNulty International, LLC. All rights reserved.

How To Become A Successful Young Man Instructor's Manual | 2016

	Name	Date	Course Day	Homework Points	Participation Y or N	Parent Participation	Daily Score
1							
2							
3							
4							
5							
6							
7							
8							
9							
10							
11							
12							
13							
14							
15							
16							
17							
18							

Pages within this book should not be reproduced without written permission from McNulty International, LLC. All rights reserved.

19							
20							
21							
22							
23							
24							
25							
26							
27							
28							
29							
30							
31							
32							
33							
34							
35							
36							
37							

Pages within this book should not be reproduced without written permission from McNulty International, LLC. All rights reserved.

How To Become A Successful Young Man Instructor's Manual | 2016

	Name	Date	Course Day	Homework Points	Participation Y or N	Parent Participation	Daily Score
1							
2							
3							
4							
5							
6							
7							
8							
9							
10							
11							
12							
13							
14							
15							
16							
17							
18							

Pages within this book should not be reproduced without written permission from McNulty International, LLC. All rights reserved.

How To Become A Successful Young Man Instructor's Manual | 2016

19							
20							
21							
22							
23							
24							
25							
26							
27							
28							
29							
30							
31							
32							
33							
34							
35							
36							
37							

Pages within this book should not be reproduced without written permission from McNulty International, LLC. All rights reserved.